Florence Nightingale

Heroes of the Cross – Mini series

Other titles in this series

Mother Teresa
Joni
Edith Cavell

Florence Nightingale

Kathleen White

Marshalls

Marshalls Paperbacks
Marshall Morgan & Scott
3 Beggarwood Lane, Basingstoke, Hants, RG23 7LP, UK

ISBN 0 551 01183 1

Phototypeset by Input Typesetting Ltd, London
Printed in Great Britain by Richard Clay
(The Chaucer Press) Ltd, Bungay, Suffolk

Contents

Introduction

Throughout history God has raised up men and women who have followed His call in a unique way. As a result of their faithfulness, God has been able to use them in remarkable ways and as a result His character and glory have been made known to many people. This series of short biographies is intended for the young person embarking on his or her reading days who wants to learn about the wealth of Christian heritage through the lives of God's people.

1:   A Privileged Home

'What delightful little daughters you have, Mrs. Nightingale,' gushed the visitor as she gazed admiringly at the two girls who had been brought by their nurse to their mother's drawing-room. 'But what unusual names you have chosen for them, quite, quite, out of the ordinary!'

Fanny Nightingale smiled fondly at both the baby in her arms and the toddler who was playing on the rug at her feet. 'Well, yes, I suppose so, but both have such happy associations for me, I wanted the children to be a reminder of the pleasure that my husband and I have found in those two places.'

Parthenope, the first child, was called by the Greek name given to her birthplace, Naples, a romantic Italian city, bathed in sunlight for most of the year, which produced sharp, tangy lemons and bright, juicy oranges, displayed to advantage against the dark green leaves of the citrus trees. A brilliant blue sky above and an incredibly blue ocean lapping on the shore completed the picture. Of course, slums existed in the narrow back streets of the old quarters but all was brightness and elegance in the area where wealthy families had their apartments.

Their younger daughter's name, Florence, would not now cause either comment or curiosity, but in 1820 when she was born it was unique. Fanny deliberately chose to stay in Florence for her second, a complete contrast to the glittering seaside city of Naples, down in the south of Italy. Wonderful art and classical buildings delighted the eyes of all the visitors who were attracted to the exciting social life in the city. When her baby daughter was born there on May 12th, 1820, her mother decided to call her after her birthplace also.

But why were Fanny and William Edward Nightingale, a wealthy upper middle-class couple from England, raising their family in Italy?

For several centuries, it had been fashionable for young noblemen or sons of rich families to undertake the 'Grand Tour' of Europe as part of their education. Towards the end of the eighteenth century, however, revolution broke out in France making journeying in that country not only difficult, but downright dangerous.

Following that, the Napoleonic Wars had further hindered communication and travel for several years so when the Battle of Waterloo in 1815 brought defeat to the French, people seized the opportunity to tour European countries once more.

Fanny and William were married in 1818; she was thirty and her husband twenty-four. The marriage was not popular with her family. Perhaps they thought the age gap of six years was on the wrong side, or maybe they feared that Fanny had taken him on the rebound after her brief romance with the impoverished, younger son of the Earl of Caithness had faded, due to lack of prospects.

Fanny had enjoyed a hectic social life with her five brothers and four sisters but in the nineteenth century, thirty was considered quite old for a woman not to be married. No doubt as the rest of the family started to grow up and leave home, Fanny wanted a family for herself and the security of marriage. She had known Williamas a boy and he could offer her a cultured mind and a prosperous background. So, although somewhat incompatible, they were married and immediately set off on an extended honeymoon of three years in Europe. Parthenope arrived in 1819 and her sister in 1820.

The Nightingales were sufficiently enlightened to enjoy having two little daughters in spite of the fact that a son would have been a great deal more convenient and secured William's inheritance for always. Probably they imagined a boy would arrive in due time as Fanny had already borne two strong, healthy children which was good for those times when infant mortality figures were very high. William's fortune came from an uncle and under the terms of his will the property reverted to his sister and eventually to her oldest son should William and Fanny fail to produce a male heir.

However, this proved to be only a small cloud on the horizon as William possessed money of his own as well. His own needs and pleasures were simple, but Fanny had aspirations to become a society hostess. With this in mind she decided to leave Italy after three years and establish a family home in England.

As his uncle's house had fallen into a very dilapidated state, William decided to build another to his own design on higher ground on the estate. So Florence at the age of one, left behind the warm country of Italy, bathed in sunshine for the major part of the year, and came to live in damp, cold Derbyshire with her sister, parents and their staff of servants.

Soon Fanny began to find fault with Lea Hurst – it was too small for their requirements, too far from London, and the climate proved unhealthy for the children. All these reasons provided her with an ideal excuse to begin house-hunting all over again, a process which dragged on for the next two years. It seemed as though no property they inspected came up to their expectations but eventually in 1825 they acquired Embley Park, near Romsey, Hampshire, just skirting the fringes of the New Forest.

At long last the Nightingales settled down happily, still spending the warmer summer months at Lea Hurst and paying occasional visits to London during the season. Both little girls flourished in their country environment. The months were filled with a round of activities. Two of Fanny's married sisters lived close by with their families so the cousins saw a great deal of each other, often coming for visits and taking Parthe and Flo back with them in return.

An ideal situation for two lively and intelligent girls, or was it? Plenty of money, youthful companionship and agreeable occupations would appear to offer a certain recipe for happiness. Fanny found it difficult to understand her younger daughter and indeed, in spite of the best intentions, Florence never formed a close association with her mother. Florence's temperament also clashed with Parthe's and would do so for most of her life.

How is it possible to gain such an intimate insight into the characters of this remarkable family? All the Nightingales and most of their relations were inveterate letter writers and a great mass of their correspondence survives today. Florence herself committed so many of her thoughts to paper. Notes to Parthe, her father or mother when she was away from home still exist to give us a detailed picture of what was going through her mind. Perhaps today letter-writing is becoming a lost art but Florence, without the benefit of such modern means of communication as the telephone, became and remained a compulsive correspondent.

Both the sisters started off with the same opportunities, the same background and loving care from parents but ended up completely dissimilar young ladies. It cannot have been easy for Parthe and it is important to be fair to her although sometimes Florence seems to gain more public sympathy, probably because of her subsequent fame. Parthe was less physically attractive than her younger sister and less capable of concentration. With her butterfly mind and sociable personality she must have been a sore trial to Florence upon occasions who was tidy, precise and neat, characteristics which would stand her in good stead later in her career.

Although Fanny only envisaged a successful future in society for her two girls, their father drew up a formidable course of study for them – Greek, Latin, German, French, Italian, history and philosophy for which he was responsible and they learnt only music and drawing from a governess. All this proved very exacting for poor Parthe who would find every excuse to slip away from her lessons. More and more Parthe identified with her mother, the successful society hostess, whereas Florence became more attached to her father whose precise, scholarly nature she shared.

Modern teenagers reading some of Florence's letters might even be excused in thinking she sounded a little priggish at times, reprimanding Parthe for her untidiness or commending herself for carrying out her mother's wishes but it was partly due to lack of worthwhile activities. By her fourteenth birthday she had acquired twenty-seven first cousins and roughly twenty-four aunts and uncles. Parthe felt fulfilled by the round of social pleasures and ceaseless comings and goings and family discussions. Florence, however, resented life spent on such a superficial level. Significantly, she revealed later on in life, 'I craved for some regular occupation, for something worth doing instead of frittering time away on useless trifles.'

It seems incredible that although her mind was being extended by so wide a range of study, her parents never planned for her to use her talents in anything more taxing than arranging a vase of flowers or sending out invitations to a dinner-party. Consequently Florence with all her abilities constantly felt frustrated as she viewed her future with apprehension.

Had she been born a hundred years later, just after the First World War, she would have stood much more of a chance of a liberal education in a girls' school with the possibility of a career afterwards. But for young ladies in her station of life, a successful marriage was the one goal to which parents aspired and for which they groomed their daughters.

One can understand Fanny's bewilderment at times when she feared she had hatched a duck-ling instead of a swan but equally it is possible to sympathise with poor Florence who longed for a purpose in life. An endearing trait in her character was her sincere affection for the little cousin who had finally put an end to William's chances of keeping his fortune in the family. Aunt Mai, William's sister, produced a son when Florence was eleven years old, but she was delighted with him and called him, 'My boy Shore,' showing no resentment or jealousy towards him. Indeed babies would always hold a very special place in Florence's heart and help to soothe and refresh her.

A piece of exciting information reached Florence in the summer when she was staying at Cowes with her sister and governess. At last their tranquil, orderly routine looked like being disturbed. William had been invited to stand as the Parliamentary candidate for Andover in the next election. To the girls it merely appeared an interesting and different project for their father, but to Fanny it held a far greater significance. After many years it seemed likely that she might realise one of her wildest dreams, a home in London. Of course, that would be absolutely essential for William to keep in close touch with the House of Commons and would further Fanny's ambition to enlarge her circle of acquaintances as a society hostess.

William thoroughly approved of the Reform

Bill of 1832 which put an end to buying votes from the electorate. In practice, when the election took place three years later, hard cash was still needed to press into many of the voters' hands to secure their support. Another candidate less scrupulous than himself was chosen and William, thoroughly disillusioned, turned his back upon politics for ever and resumed the even tenor of his life as a country gentleman.

Fanny, however, was not content to slip back into the old ways. Deprived of her permanent entry into London society, she threw herself wholeheartedly into launching her two daughters in the fashionable world. Embley would serve as the base for all the entertainment necessary for their coming-out but in its present form it would need extensive rebuilding and alterations before it would be adequate for the grandiose schemes Fanny had in mind.

She found an unexpected ally in William who once again looked forward to producing architectural plans as he had done before at Lea Hurst. To save expense over this period, the Nightingales decided to close down both their establishments in England and travel on the continent until the work was completed. Everyone in the family was delighted. William looked forward to meeting old friends, Fanny to buying clothes in

Paris and generally enjoying the social whirl. Both the girls had been far too young to remember anything of their previous sojourn in Europe. So it was with a sense of adventure that they contemplated the whole trip.

William's creative genius again sprang to the fore when he drew designs for a handsome new travelling coach to convey the members of the family inside and the servants sitting on seats on the roof. Six horses were needed to pull the contraption so it must have aroused a great deal of notice and comment as it bowled along the country roads of France and Italy. But just before they set out on this momentous journey a most important event happened in Florence's life which eventually would change the whole of her outlook and her future.

After all, had she not written, '. . . since I was six, I had craved to have something to do, a profession, a trade, something to fill and employ all my faculties.' How was this to be brought about?

2:   A Voice Heard

For some years, then, Florence had felt a vague dissatisfaction with her lifestyle. Her material surroundings were all that she could have wanted but always there was something lacking, a sense of purpose, a challenge, motivation for the future – a vague emptiness. Then totally unexpectedly, Florence received a call from God.

'On February 7th, 1837, God spoke to me and called me to His service.' This simple statement of fact was written down in one of her private notebooks without any fancy embroidery of words which one might have expected in such a surprising situation. One thing became quite clear, it was a voice speaking to her from an outside source and not merely her imagination working overtime.

Many people over the centuries, including Joan of Arc, have made the same claim. But Florence heard the voice of God more than once. We have her written record that these so-called voices spoke to her distinctly on three other occasions: in 1853 before she took up her first post at the Hospital for Poor Gentlewomen in Harley Street, again before her service in the Crimea in 1854, and finally after her friend and associate, Sidney Herbert, died in 1861.

In some ways, it must have seemed a somewhat unclear call as she had no idea exactly what task God was asking her to perform. At that stage nursing held no special place in her life. It might even have appeared an odd time for God to make her aware of His claims on her when she was just about to set out on an extended holiday. Florence herself did not question the experience, it gave her an inner peace and assurance which she had hitherto lacked although a long period would elapse before its true significance would dawn on her.

So, hugging this secret in her heart, Florence set off with the rest of her family to Southampton en route for France on September 8th, 1837. Far from being preoccupied by her recent call, she went into raptures about the European scenery and the beautiful old buildings, recording all her adventures in her diary and adding details also in her letters, particularly to her cousin, Hilary Bonham Carter.

Travelling to Nice, then Genoa and Florence, the Nightingales entered fully into the social life of every city in which they stopped. Fanny rented a magnificent apartment in the centre of fashionable Florence and privately patted herself on the back at the success of her plan. Her younger daughter was developing a passion for dancing and was making quite an impact on Italian notables. 'Florence was much noticed,' she wrote with brevity but great satisfaction in a letter to her sister. Indeed, with her trained mind, Florence was instantly attracted to many aspects of Italian culture, the music, literature and art.

At that time the struggle for Italian nationalism was being strongly opposed by Austria. When the Nightingales moved on to Geneva, they met many political refugees who had been persecuted by the Austrians. Florence became an ardent advocate of freedom for the repressed country of her birth. Suddenly a political crisis blew up forcing the family to leave Geneva sooner than they desired. The French were threatening to declare war on the Swiss because Louis Napolean

Bonaparte had been given sanctuary there to visit his dying mother.

Just as suddenly the crisis died down, but not before the Nightingales had left for Paris to the sound of barricades being erected and trenches dug in the streets. There Florence not only revelled in all the social attractions but made friends with many intellectuals as well, including one Mary Clarke in particular – her beloved 'Clarkey' of later years.

After eighteen months abroad, they crossed the Channel once more to take up residence at Embley. Florence's mind was a turmoil of emotions, full of happy memories of her triumphs in European society but conscience-stricken that it was now two years since God had spoken to her and she had done nothing about it. Like many other outstanding reformers she found it a hard struggle to renounce her natural enjoyment in worldly pleasure. 'My first temptation to overcome is my desire to shine in society,' she confessed in a private note, just as Elizabeth Fry herself a pioneer in prison reform, had found to her cost in her younger days. Fanny possessed no inkling of this conflict in Florence's mind. She was merely delighted at her social success. The prospect for her daughter's future looked bright indeed. Perhaps Florence was beginning to conform.

Both Florence and Parthe were presented at the Queen's birthday drawing room. A full calendar of social events filled every moment. Further complications arose when Florence became extremely attached to her cousin Marianne Nicholson. Her brother Henry fell in love with Florence who certainly didn't return his affection but unfortunately encouraged him in order to see more of Marianne.

The return to Embley was fraught with difficulties because the workmen fell behind in their schedule. However, even Fanny was satisfied at last with the magnificent furnishings and redecorations and held a huge house-warming party at Christmas to show off its splendour to her friends and relations.

The balloon of life deflated again. Florence worried about her relations with Henry and her lack of response to God's call. A visit to her beloved Aunt Mai restored both her health and spirits somewhat. She was even allowed to indulge in a few mathematics lessons to occupy her mind but as Fanny said, 'What use are mathematics to a married woman?' This was Fanny's sole objective for Florence.

Another young man, Richard Monkton Milnes, began to take an interest in Florence, but she by this time was finding another outlet for her energies. By 1842, the period in English history called the hungry forties was causing untold distress. Florence saw a little of it when she visited the desperately poor hovels in the villages with gifts of food and money, particularly at Lea Hurst. Fanny soon lost patience with her although she herself was generous to the poor. Florence was not merely content to play 'Lady Bountiful', she begged for medicines and old linen to make bandages.

Two years later her mind cleared and she knew for certain what God was calling her to perform but she could not share her vision with her parents. Various short nursing assignments came her way, looking after a dead friend's baby and caring for her dear cousin Shore recovering from measles. Later she also stayed with her grand-mother and then her old nurse while they were ill, a little compensation to her while she was suffering great mental anguish after refusing Henry Nicholson's proposal. This of course meant she had to forfeit Marianne's friendship which was very distressing for her.

Fourteen years in all were to elapse before she could take up nursing. At first she enjoyed just caring for sick people as a concerned amateur but she soon realised she needed proper training, charity was not sufficient. 'Mama was terrified,' she wrote to a cousin when the subject was first mooted of Florence working in a hospital. Distressing family scenes took place and once more Florence's spirits plummeted to the depth. 'It was as if I had wanted to be a kitchenmaid,' she wrote.

One cannot altogether blame the Nightingales for their attitude to nursing. They merely knew of hospitals as filthy and overcrowded squalid buildings. Patients also were usually dirty and quite often drunk. Today's nurses are immaculately clean and hygienic, but in Florence's youth just about the only women who would undertake nursing duties were immoral and addicted to drink themselves. Small wonder Fanny refused to contemplate this career for her daughter!

Anyone of a weaker character would have relinquished her ambition long ago. Florence was torn apart by the conflict in her life, between her call by God and her duty to her parents. '. . . forgive me . . . and let me die, oh Lord,' she even wrote once. The petty routine of her daily existence irked her increasingly until she took another positive step. She began to rise early in the morning and pore over reports on Hospitals and Public Health. Then she summarised the essential facts in notebooks which she hid in her room. Outwardly she remained the dutiful younger daughter helping with the running of the household, but she was slowly building up her inner mental reserves.

A kindly friend rescued her and took her abroad to Italy for a while. There she first met Sidney Herbert who was to play such a large part in her life. He and his wife as enlightened Christians encouraged her research into hospital reform but she had to be content with teaching in a Ragged School at Westminster and visiting sick cottagers. Fanny became furious when she turned down Richard Milnes' offer of marriage and once more she escaped her mother's wrath by travelling abroad with a friend.

The emotional tug-of-war continued as we glimpse in her diaries. 'Now Lord, let me think only of Thy Will, what then willest me to do.' A quick visit to the institute for Protestant Deaconesses in Karserwerth, Germany, strengthened her resolve. Parthe tried to cling like a leech to her, demanding all her attention. Henry Nicholson died of a drowning tragedy in Spain and Richard Monkton Milnes became engaged to someone else, tired of waiting for Florence to make up her mind.

In the summer of 1851 she spent several months at Karserwerth where she helped with the children and even was present at some operations. She formed a close friendship with Herr Fliedner and his wife and they in turn had nothing but praise for the way in which she had gone about her duties. 'We were all taught to pray aloud . . . in front of the whole community whenever it was called for,' she commented years later. In spite of such a dedicated background Fanny still did not approve and when Florence wrote asking, 'Give me your blessing,' she remained silent.

All this time Florence was building up a circle of influential and distinguished friends, among whom were Elizabeth Barrett Browning, George Eliot, Lord Shaftesbury and Lord Palmerston. She won her father's sympathy but even he was afraid of open confrontation with his wife. Florence escaped once more to a meeting of the British Association in Belfast but was recalled home as Parthe had suffered a breakdown. In 1853 she managed a visit to Paris to inspect a hospital run by the Sisters of Charity and then drew up long detailed reports on the organisation.

Finally Florence had to take matters into her own hands. Through Sidney Herbert's wife Liz she heard of a medical Establishment for Gentlewomen which needed a Superintendent.

She was interviewed, and accepted for the post by people who thought highly of her. 'I am sure she must be a most remarkable person,' wrote Lady Canning. Once more she had to try to sell the idea to her family – and failed. But this time she was adamant and took over the Institution with all its muddle and short-comings. It was to be a marvellous training-ground for the nightmare that lay ahead, as yet unforeseen.

When the Committee appointed Florence, most of the members held a romantic view of her, expecting her to act rather like a benevolent, presiding angel. Florence amazed and even shocked some of them. She insisted on accepting patients from all denominations, not just Church of England communicants. As the finances had been left in a deplorable muddle, she decided to review the whole system of ordering and paying bills. She made constant innovations, introducing new methods and inventions which would save her over-worked nurses. Dirty rooms and equipment were cleaned; filthy bed-linen and furnishings were thrown out.

Out of the £500 a year she received from her father, Florence paid for many extras for her grateful patients. One of the main problems at the Institute was to get them discharged.

Most, even when fully recovered in health, wanted to stay on indefinitely because of the wonderful kindness and comfort they were given.

One might have expected that all Florence's energies would be absorbed in this challenging situation, but once she had dealt with the outstanding deficiencies in the Institution she began to draw up reports on reforming hospitals. Here she met with both jealousy and indifference, foreshadowing the attitude of many officials during her period in the Crimea, incredible as it may seem to us. It gradually dawned on her that the most pressing need was to set up training schools for nurses.

During a cholera epidemic which broke out in London, Florence worked as a volunteer for the Middlesex Hospital, personally caring for filthy women off the streets and applying their bandages herself.

In vain Fanny remonstrated and remarked tearfully, 'We are ducks who have hatched a wild swan.' Nothing would stop Florence now she had found out God's purpose for her life. She could never return to the petty socialising of Lea Hurst and Embley.

Events were about to bring dramatic change to Florence's life again. All the toil and effort she had endured in Harley Street would appear child's play compared with the mammoth task that Florence would be asked to shoulder.

3: Why No Nurses?

After less than a year in Harley Street, Florence, like the rest of the nation, heard that Britain and France had declared war on Russia. Only a few months to become used to organisation and decision-making and yet it must have seemed a life-time away from the beautiful gowns, lovely drawing-rooms and soft music of her parents' world of polite society!

At first the news made little impact on most British citizens apart from arousing in their hearts a fervour of patriotism and a certainty that before long their troops would once more be crowned with the laurels of military success. To think otherwise was treason – but even within the space of a few short weeks the unthinkable began to happen.

Forty years had elapsed since the Battle of Waterloo, when the British army had achieved the impossible and defeated the legendary Napoleon. Full of confidence the nation unquestionably imagined that after a few short but decisive skirmishes their soldiers would sail home again triumphing in glory. What people failed to realise was that the whole army had been allowed to run down and the machinery of war in every department was hopelessly diminished.

As so often in a long period of peace, the government had become complacent and allowed stringent economies to take place. Just as in the next century it would be found there was a general unpreparedness in both the government and the armed services to face two devastating World Wars, so in the Spring of 1854 the amount of men, stores and equipment would prove to be laughable. Virtually no transport system existed to convey the army and its vast stores of necessities. Only a comparative handful of clerks tried to cope with the million and one jobs connected with mobilising and equipping a whole army.

The Cabinet was divided even upon the need to go to war. Lord Aberdeen still hoped to achieve peace by negotiation, but he was overruled after a Turkish flotilla had been destroyed by the main Russian fleet off Sinope, in the Black Sea.

'Why have women passion, intellect, moral activity – these three – and a place in society where not one of the three can be exercised?' had been Florence Nightingale's indignant cry in the past. But now there had arisen a situation which would call for all these qualities and forever change the concept of the place of women in British Society.

At the start of the campaign, the first objective of the British army was to relieve Silistria in Rumania where the Russians were besieging the Turks. The main base was established at Scutari on the Asian shore of the Bosphorus. Troops from England who had disembarked in June, 1854, became victims not to the terrible wounds of war but the equally terrible scourge of cholera. Weakened and debilitated, they hung on until the Turks raised the siege of Silistria and then joined the rest of the Allied forces in the main objective of wiping out the huge Russian naval base at Sebastopol.

This necessitated re-embarking at Varna in Bulgaria and setting sail for the Crimean peninsula. The supply of boats was so inadequate that virtually most of the medical equipment and stores had to be left behind. Thirty thousand

34

men were crammed in the boats but when they landed at Calamita Bay of ill-omened name, many of them were still suffering from cholera and Army doctors possessed very little medication to stem the tide of the disease.

A victory gained by the British and French troops at the Battle of the Alma raised the morale of the British nation even higher at home, but wreaked terrible havoc amongst the troops actually involved in the fighting. One thousand cholera cases already had been sent back to Scutari; they were soon to be joined by a thousand more. The wounded who had survived the battle lay around on the filthy ground without dressings or morphia. Florence later was to be known in this area as 'the Lady with the lamp' but the surgeons who preceded her there only had the benefit of the moonlight by which to work, performing amputations without an anaesthetic.

Any soldier who was fortunate to survive this treatment eventually was sent to the old Turkish barracks at Scutari. Hopelessly inadequate from the start with appalling drains and sanitary arrangements, it became filled to crisis point with cholera victims and battle casualties as the original British hospital was already crammed to overflowing.

Even the journey across the Black Sea in dangerously crowded transport ships brought almost as much risk to the soldiers as the battle itself. If they arrived alive, more often than not they lay in long rows on the filthy floors, still wrapped in the blood-stained blankets which had been thrown round them after they were wounded. Not only was there precious little medication or doctors, there were not even common necessities like beds, chairs or cups, and the lack of a proper kitchen made the preparation of food impossible.

In a sense, this was no new situation for the unfortunate soldiery. Conditions had always been not just inadequate but often horrific for men wounded in previous campaigns. However, such information did not stir the conscience of the nation because it never filtered through to them. Communications up to the Crimean War had been painfully slow so the full horror story never reached the country as a whole at the time.

However, at the beginning of the Crimean campaign an innovation took place. The Times newspaper sent out the first war correspondent, William Howard Russell. Thoroughly unpopular and unwelcome from the start with the army authorities, his forthright and revealing dispatches after the battle of Alma stirred

England. 'No sufficient preparations have been made for the care of the wounded, not only not sufficient surgeons; not only no dressers and nurses; but not even enough linen to make bandages.' For the first time the British people heard the unpalatable truth, 'Not only are the men kept . . . sometimes for a week without a medical man coming near their wounds . . . and left to expire in agony but now it is found the commonest appliances of the workhouse sick ward are lacking . . .'

Although the army authorities tried to bluster and cover up the situation, it became apparent that the French had made excellent arrangements for the care of their sick and wounded, having brought with them many dedicated Sisters of Charity to act as nurses. And so, the cry that rang round the nation by October was, 'Why have we no Sisters of Charity?'

Already a Times fund had been opened to supply comforts to the men. But official sanction at the top was needed for radical reform. Fortunately Sidney Herbert had been made Secretary for War two years previously and he sprang into immediate action telling the British Ambassador at Constantinople to buy anything he considered necessary.

He also took an even more important step in

writing to Florence to ask her to travel to Scutari with a party of nurses, sanctioned and financed by the Government. In one sense, he was too late as she had already decided to go. Her invitation was ratified by the Cabinet. Unfortunately she was only described as Superintendent of the Female Establishment of the English General Military Hospitals in Turkey, which made it difficult for her to work in the Crimea later.

It is amusing to read how her fickle family, who had opposed her at every turn, now went into raptures about her appointment. Choosing her staff of nurses proved extremely difficult. In the end she engaged fourteen professional nurses and the other twenty-four all came from religious bodies. Florence quite firmly stated that everyone, whatever her social status, would be treated exactly the same. The only difference was that the nuns and sisters were still allowed to wear their habits and the rest were clothed in a very ugly uniform.

The party travelled via France where they were given a rapturous reception. Unfortunately the weather became atrocious when they embarked at Marseilles. Florence suffered terribly from seasickness throughout the voyage and must have felt wretched as she arrived at the Barrack Hospital which was a pity, as even someone of the most robust stamina would flinch at the sight that met her eyes.

Each side of the hospital was nearly a quarter of a mile long. The fourth side had been destroyed by fire. Even then Florence reckoned there were four miles of beds. Yet she and her staff had been allocated just six rooms altogether, filthy, damp, with very little furniture and no food. Water was strictly rationed to one pint a head per day for both washing and drinking. The body of a Russian general occupied one of the rooms.

A less determined person than Florence would have travelled back home as soon as possible with such a welcome. But Florence had been trained in a hard school. Only by force of will-power had she reached her present situation. It seems incredible that at each stage of her career she had to fight to establish her ideas, first her family, next the Army authorities, and lastly many of the various Government departments. It is hard for people today to understand the opposition she met.

Far from being delighted by her arrival, military and medical officers, jealous of her popularity, put every stumbling-block they could in her way. Ironically she had been assured by the War Office that 'nothing is wanted at Scutari'.

In the end Florence became, in her own words, 'a kind of General Dealer; in socks, shirts, knives and forks, wooden spoons, tin baths, tables and forms, cabbages and carrots, operating tables, towels and soap, small tooth combs, precipitate for destroying lice, scissors, bedpans and stump pillows.'

Florence's mission fell quite naturally into two distinct divisions. The first dealt with the fearsome emergency which was already building up before she arrived and raged throughout the winter of 1854–55. In a sense, she was powerless to stem the collapse of the whole administration until she had established herself and her nurses, and had received acceptance from the stubborn military authorities. To achieve this she worked day and night for several weeks under impossible conditions.

The second spell took place from the Spring of 1855 until her return to England in the summer of 1856. Altogether she spent a relatively short time out in the Crimean area but it had far-reaching effects, far more than the instant alleviation of the soldiers' traumatic sufferings. It began a complete overhaul of the whole question of military hospitals and perhaps even more important, made a profound change in the training of nurses for the future. Sidney Herbert wrote to her before she left, 'If this succeeds, an enormous amount of good will have been done now . . . a prejudice will have been broken through and a precedent established which will multiply the good to all time.'

Strangely enough some of the first opposition came from her own nurses. Expecting a heroine's welcome, they were rebuffed and ignored and given petty jobs like sorting linen and counting stores. Florence realised that they could only start on their main work, that of nursing the terribly sick and wounded, when they were clearly accepted by the doctors in charge.

It is a long and incredible story. The first foothold Florence gained was in the kitchens. The kitchen utensils and cooking equipment hardly existed and the men, if they were lucky, drank greasy water in which unappetising pieces of meat had been thrown. Florence began cooking arrowroot, serving a little wine for medicinal purposes and warming beef essences for men who were severely ill. She must have been desperate to begin her real work, but she never lost her self-control with the maddening hospital staff. 'She was always calm and self-possessed,' said one of her nurses. 'She was a perfect lady through everything – never overbearing. I never heard her raise her voice.'

Again the same nurse wrote, 'For a week after our arrival, we were occupied . . . in making shirts, pillow strings . . . then we filled coarse wrappers with chopped straw . . . and then sewed up the fourth side and thus completed the pallet.' So with a few delicacies of food and a rough mattress between them and the hard, cold floor, the men must have started to count their blessings.

And so it might have gone on indefinitely but fresh fighting started off a major emergency of gigantic proportions, so serious that the doctors and administrators put their grudges behind them and gladly co-operated with Florence and her nurses. The atrocious weather had made the countryside a nightmare of mud and squalor. Finally the Russians attacked at Inkerman on November 5th. One cannot altogether blame the doctors, they were submerged by a sea of paperwork, signing and counter-signing for every item. They were totally unprepared for this further calamity.

Another aggravation was the smell of sickness and decay mingled with the smell of drains. Underneath the hospital 'were sewers . . . loaded with filth, mere cesspools, though which the wind blew sewer air up the pipes of open privies in the corridors where the sick were lying.'

On the night of November 14th there arose the worst storm the Crimea had ever known and the ship, Prince, laden with comforts for the wounded and valuable stores of every description, went down with twenty-seven other vessels and sank in Balaclava harbour.

4: 'We Could Kiss Her Shadow'

Hospital officials finally tumbled to the fact that Florence had a great deal of money at her disposal in this dire extremity, much of which had been collected by her personally. With the help of several able young men appointed to her staff, she rented a house outside the barracks and arranged for the washing to be done by the soldiers' wives. The previous record of 'six shirts washed a month' for two thousand sick soldiers hardly seemed adequate to her. More than two hundred and sixty women and children lived in the dark cellars underneath the hospital. Children and adults were separated and a regular food supply instituted for all.

Over Christmas, Queen Victoria sent gifts to the men and a personal message to Florence which strengthened her position amongst the officials. The common soldiers loved her already. Often she was on her feet for twenty four hours at a stretch. People saw her on her knees dressing wounds for eight hours on end. Her only accommodation was a bed behind a screen in a storeroom. She suffered dreadfully from the cold and damp. Yet she found time to stand by them and comfort them on the dreaded operation table. 'What a comfort it was to see her pass even', a soldier wrote home. '. . . we lay there by hundreds; but we could kiss her shadow as it fell and lay our heads on the pillow again content.'

Florence had the latrines emptied and hired Turkish labourers to build up the fourth side of the hospital which had been burnt down. Then she prepared for the avalanche of wounded, carried down the muddy heights from the battle and conveyed in agony in boats tossing on the wintry sea. The dysentery cases died at the rate of one in two. In the first winter she estimated she had witnessed over 2,000 deaths. By January 1855 there were 12,000 men in hospital and only 11,000 in the trenches, and still the death-rate was on the increase.

In spite of her many duties, Florence did not

spare herself from any menial jobs which her band of nurses was carrying out, she made time to write letters for her soldiers and her staff to their loved ones at home. She also scribbled copious notes and detailed reports to Sidney Herbert describing at first-hand the problems she encountered daily. Although this extra work was a drain on her ebbing strength, it nevertheless fanned the flame of resentment and discontent at home against the military organisation.

As a result the government was forced to set up two Commissions of Enquiry. One, called the McNeill and Tulloch Commission, was given the task of examining the whole system of supplies for the British Army in the Crimea. The other one, led by a Dr. Sutherland, was to investigate the sanitary state of the field hospitals. From both sides, Florence won valuable friends who would prove a staunch support to her in her future work.

The latter landed in Scutari in March and immediately set about establishing a clean, safe, water supply. They got rid of much of the vermin, cleaned the sewers and limewashed the walls. Needless to say, the death-rate fell. Not only had the actual conditions improved, but the soldiers' morale as well. No longer were they being brought to the hospital merely to die of filth and neglect.

Food was marvellously improved when a famous chef named Alexis Soyer arrived. He insisted on training proper army cooks and made nourishing soup and stews with the men's rations. Heartened by the progress that had been made in so many departments, Florence decided to visit the two large hospitals in the Crimea. Dr. Hall, her old adversary from Scutari, tried to make it as difficult as possible for her and stirred up trouble with the nurses in residence.

She arrived on May 5th, 1855, but had only been there two days before she was struck down with a virulent fever which nearly cost her her life. Although Dr. Hall wanted to ship her back to England to convalesce out of the way she insisted on being left back at Scutari. Undoubtedly, the long, enforced rest saved her life. Florence would have been excused had she decided to give up her work at that stage but, convinced she was obeying the call of God she had heard under such different circumstances, she was determined to carry on. 'If I go, all this will go to pieces,' she wrote to Parthe.

In October she travelled back to the Crimea a second time to carry out the tasks left undone by her illness. Her health was permanently affected by this time and she came in for a great deal of criticism about her nurses. Again she had to leave for Scutari as a new cholera epidemic had broken out. But at home her prestige was never higher. A Nightingale Fund was set up in her honour and Queen Victoria presented her with a brooch designed by Prince Albert, bearing the message 'Blessed are the merciful'.

Florence never set out to court popularity and therefore did not become inflated by the money and honours bestowed upon her. Fanny, however, gained great satisfaction from the national aclamation, '. . . the most interesting day of thy mother's life . . . the like has never happened before, but will, I trust, from your example gladden the hearts of many future mothers' – rather an ironic comment after all the opposition to Florence's chosen career!

Refusing to rest on her laurels, Florence set herself fresh targets to achieve. Now the worst faults in the hospital had been cleared up, and a wounded man brought in there could expect a bed, clean clothing, nourishing food and medical attention, she turned to alleviating the lot of the ordinary common soldier. Although strenuously opposed by the authorities, she opened a small reading-room for convalescent soldiers. Discovering that many could neither read or write, she tried to engage a schoolmaster but this was flatly refused. Next she struggled for facilities for the men to remit some of their pay home to their families. £71,000 was sent home in less than six months. 'It is all money saved from the drink shops,' said Florence.

Then she opened a recreation room supplied with newspapers, writing materials and games. The officers warned her that the men would steal the notepaper and sell it for drink, but in this they were proved totally wrong. 'The men,' she wrote, '. . . could not have presented a more silent or orderly scene.'

Eventually she was able to make the authorities change their minds and four schools were opened. Singing classes were formed and amateur theatricals took place. Outdoor games for the fit and board games for the invalids were in great demand. One onlooker commented, 'She taught officers and officials to treat the soldiers as Christian men.' A revolution had taken place; the British soldier would never again be classed as a drunken brute. It was only through Florence's persistence in the face of hostile opposition that the British Army gradually acquired its NAAFIs, and splendid leisure facilities that have become an integral part of the system today.

All this, of course, was at the expense of her health. 'They are killing me,' she told Aunt Mai who had come out to join her. The bitter cold of another Crimean winter was taking its toll of her, she was suffering from earache and continued laryngitis. Aunt Mai in her turn reported on Florence's situation, 'She continually writes till one or two, sometimes till three or four . . . You would be surprised at the temperatures in which she lives, she who suffers so much from cold.'

In spite of Florence's single-minded and unselfish devotion, enemies were still at work to undermine her reputation. When the final report of the McNeill and Tulloch Commission was published, far from the men responsible for the atrocious muddle and criminal negligence being demoted, a great whitewashing process began and two of the worst opponents to Florence in the hospital received knighthoods, one of them the bigoted Dr. John Hall.

Florence was absolutely furious – not for herself but for the sheer injustice of the whole concern. 'I am in a state of chronic rage,' she wrote in March 1856, 'I who saw the men come down through all that long dreadful winter, without other covering than a dirty blanket and a pair of old regimental trousers, when we knew the stores were bursting with warm clothing, living skeletons devoured by vermin, ulcerated, hopeless, speechless . . . Can we hear of the promotions of the men who caused this colossal calamity, we who saw it? Would that the men could speak who died in the puddles of Calamita Bay!'

Florence's righteous indignation lent fire to her words. There had existed a serious lack of many kinds of essential equipment, right from the start. That had been galling enough on its own but it was even more frustrating for her to discover that tons of warm clothing and other vital supplies were denied to the heroes fighting in impossible conditions because the necessary paperwork had not been completed.

She was not merely writing exaggerated claims from hearsay, she had actually been at the front and witnessed it for herself. After her first visit to Balaclava she wrote, 'Fancy working five nights out of seven in the trenches! Fancy being 36 hours in them at a stretch . . . lying down . . . after 48 hours with no food but raw salt pork sprinkled with sugar, rum and biscuit; nothing hot because the exhausted soldier could not collect his own fuel, as he was expected to do, to cook his own ration . . .'

Florence had alleviated many of the worst sufferings by the time the report came out but the sting remained. She identified with the common soldier not the officials mismanaging the whole campaign. Later, on her return home, she would write, 'No one can feel for the Army as I do. These people who talk to us have all fed their children on the fat of the land and dressed them in velvet and silk, while we have been away. I have had to see my children dressed in a dirty blanket and an old pair of regimental trousers, and to see them fed on raw salt meat, and nine thousand of my children are lying, from causes which might have been prevented, in their forgotten graves.'

In a desperate letter to Sidney Herbert she stated, 'The War Office gives me tinsel and plenty of praise, which I do not want, and does not give me the real businesslike efficient standing which I do want.' She still had to wait until March for proper recognition. General Orders finally admitted her sole and complete responsibility for all the nurses in the military hospitals in the Army. If only it had come earlier!

Although peace talks had already started in Paris, she again travelled to Balaclava, arriving in a blinding snowstorm. Frustrated with the ever-lasting form-filling, she had to feed her nurses at her own expense. To visit two of the outlying hospitals, she was exposed to severe cold and snow, all of which took toll of her failing health.

Peace was proclaimed on April 29th, but it brought little comfort to Florence who was desperately afraid that army life would slip back into the old chaos once the emergency had died down. 'Believe me when I say that everything in the Army (in point of routine versus system) is just where it was eighteen months ago . . .'

Back in Scutari, she busied herself in tidying up the hospital until July when the last patient was taken off by transport for home. In England, her reputation was never higher. In the House of Lords, she was described as '. . . an angel of mercy . . . who still lingers . . . at the scene of her labours . . . at Scutari where dying men sat up to catch the sound of her footsteps or the flutter of her dress.'

The whole grateful nation was agog to pay honour to her. She had captured everyone's imagination. Wives and mothers longed to shower gratitude on her. To convey her home in a suitable manner, the Government offered to send a man-of-war. Regiments planned fitting tributes to her and all sorts of ceremonials were planned for her arrival at Lea Hurst.

Nothing could have been further from Florence's wishes. Her thoughts and memories were still with her 'poor children', those men who would never come home from the war. 'Oh my poor men, I am a bad mother to come home and leave you in your Crimean graves – 73 per cent in eight regiments in six months from disease alone – who thinks of that now?'

She and Aunt Mai travelled incognito as Mrs. and Miss Smith on a boat to Marseilles. Florence arrived alone in England, spent one day at the Convent of the Bermondsey Nuns and then turned up, unheralded at Lea Hurst, walking up from the station.

Although she had been responsible for a revolution, she was obsessed by depression and failure, what might have been accomplished. Florence would never forget her dreadful ordeal in the Crimea.

5: The Lamp Still Burns

Florence had never tried to stir up public acclaim for herself and dismissed it all as mere 'buz fuz'. So naturally, far from being sympathetic to plans to honour her achievements in the Crimea, her sole objective was to achieve fresh concessions and further advantages for the soldiers who had survived the war. 'I stand at the altar of the murdered man,' she wrote, 'and while I live I fight for their cause.'

She knew well that she must strike while the iron was hot. Public memory was notoriously short and fickle. Humanly speaking she was worn out; she had become ill and exhausted after her strenuous efforts out in Scutari. Her main aim in life had been realised in tending the sick. With this she would have been still content but the urgency of the situation drove her on to take up her pen and press for reform. She would have preferred to shun the limelight but somebody must tackle the problem.

Floods of letters and gifts poured in. All were acknowledged by Parthe but Florence gave no interviews, signed no autographs and made no public appearances. She would have been justified in exploiting her popularity to further her ends, but that was not her way. But how was she to achieve her aims?

An unexpected summons from the Queen to give a first-hand account of her experiences during the war injected her with fresh energy. Here was a golden opportunity not to be missed. Although the Queen herself had little power, she held a strong influence on public opinion. Florence knew that the same sort of catastrophe could easily arise again unless there was a complete overhaul of the whole army system. She planned to ask for a Royal Commission 'to examine the sanitary condition, administration and organisation of barracks and military hospitals and the organisation, education and administration of the Army Medical Department.' A tall order indeed, but every detail was necessary for the welfare of the private soldier both in peace and in war.

Florence did her homework meticulously before she travelled to Scotland. Prince Albert, she knew, would expect accurate statistics and a wealth of information. Her diligence was well rewarded. The royal couple listened attentively and on several occasions she was invited back to Balmoral for further discussions. The Prince wrote, '. . . We are much pleased with her; she is extremely modest.' The Queen declared herself even more strongly. 'I wish we had her at the War Office,' she confided to the Duke of Cambridge.

Delay proved inevitable as the War Office was reluctant to authorise such an enquiry, fearing what scandals it might uncover. Finally, the Commission was set up in May 1857, with Florence's old friend, Sidney Herbert, as chairman. Florence pushed herself to the utmost of her physical limits. She became involved in interviewing people and writing reams of evidence. Apart from her work connected with the Commission, Florence somehow found time to write a 1000 page volume about the army medical system, Notes on Matters affecting the Health, Efficiency and Hospital Administration of the British Army.

All this would have been a strain for Florence

in her poor state of health even under ideal conditions. As it was, Florence had taken up her headquarters in the Burlington Hotel which would be central for her work but Fanny and Parthe refused to be parted from her, basking in her reflected glory. Their petty occupations and socialising nearly drove her insane. 'The whole occupation of Parthe and Mama was to lie on two sofas and tell one another not to get tired by putting flowers into water,' complained Florence later in a letter to a friend. Florence travelled to Malvern to recuperate for a while after collapsing. When she returned to London, she did so as an invalid and for the rest of her life worked mainly from her bed.

Happily for the family, a new interest gave them fresh occupation. Parthe became engaged to Sir Harry Verney, an M.P. and pioneer in social reform. This not only gave Fanny worthwhile employment but effectually moved Parthe from being an encumbrance to Florence. Florence herself expected she would soon die, she felt so ill. She made her will and entrusted Sidney Herbert with the job of making sure the conditions of the Commission were implemented.

Strangely enough she was to live for over another fifty years. Although she had become a legend in her own lifetime, many people were unaware that she still existed. Shut away from the public gaze, she carried on her philanthropic work only coming in contact with a comparative handful of people. She had even offered to join the troops when the Indian Mutiny broke out in 1857 but Sidney Herbert dissuaded her owing to her state of health.

Eventually she was able to perform a great service for the country of India by drafting a Circular of Enquiry and some further Observations which were published in 1862, underlining the troubles in that country. For years the annual death-rate in the Indian Army had been 69 per 1,000, an unacceptable 'high'. Pressing for sanitary reform for the troops, she realised she would need to agitate for new sanitary standards for the whole nation. Although she never visited India herself, she was considered an undisputed authority on many aspects of Indian affairs and officials often called on her before taking up appointments on Indian soil. She campaigned also for irrigation schemes to alleviate starvation in the villages, new and fairer forms of taxation and the right for Indians to enter the Civil Service. The amount of reports and statistics she produced on the vast subject was absolutely staggering.

But before that, in 1859, she published Notes on Hospitals explaining her ideas about hospital organisation and construction, very much ahead of its time. The same year saw the appearance of another short book by her, Notes on Nursing: What it is and what it is not. It was quickly sold out and reprinted on several occasions, being full of sound, practical common-sense.

Although a grateful nation had contributed to a 'Nightingale Fund' of £45,000, it was a source of embarrassment to Florence who had no wish to make use of it for her own personal gain. A subject close to her heart was the establishment of a training school for nurses and, after some deliberation, this was what she set up with the help of the Fund. 'It seems to me to be the best possible. It will be beginning in a very humble way,' she wrote.

Already familiar with St. Thomas's Hotpital and having full confidence in its matron Mrs. Wardropen, she decided to start her school there. Naturally, there was some opposition from various quarters at such an innovation but in spite of setbacks, the school finally opened in July 1860 with fifteen probationers. The moral aspect of the nurses' training was held to be almost as important as the technical. If a nurse passed the strict interview, she had to keep a daily diary which Florence read at the end of the month. By today's standards this appears a great infringement of personal liberty but we have to remember the poor reputation of nurses up to the Crimean War and the necessity for Florence to elevate the profession to a proper standard.

Unfortunately, Florence was as demanding on other co-workers as she was on her own frail but indomitable body. Refusing to accept that Sidney Herbert's had broken down, she goaded him on to fresh efforts on behalf of the British soldier but he died in 1861 murmuring, 'Poor Florence . . . poor Florence – our joint work unfinished.'

It took her a long time to recover from Sidney Herbert's death. She was beset by remorse at the way she had made no concessions for his sickness. Gradually, though, other thoughts and plans occupied her energies. She became involved in the workhouse system and Poor Law reform, district nursing and childbirth statistics. From her couch were sent letters and reports all over the world and she became known as an authority over a wide range of such matters. Henri Dunant, who himself was the founder of the International Red Cross after he had been horrified at the treatment of wounded soldiers on the battlefield, paid tribute to her. 'Though I am known as the founder of the Red Cross and the originator of the Convention of Geneva, it is to an Englishwoman that all the honour of the Convention is due. What inspired me was the work of Miss Florence Nightingale in the Crimea.'

She kept in touch with many of her nurses on training and often sent them delicacies if they were ill or invited them to stay if she considered they needed a rest and a change. Her main diversions were babies whom she loved and cats, often working with a cat 'tied in a knot round her neck.' Her faith afforded her great comfort. 'Religion is not devotion but work and suffering for the love of God.' Even as early as 1885 she wrote on Christmas Day when she was sixty-five, 'Today, Oh Lord, let me dedicate this crumbling old woman to Thee.' Yet the Lord was going to use this fragile vessel for another twenty-five years to be a help and inspiration to many far younger people who witnessed her shining example of unselfish service.

Gradually results were achieved, not as quickly as she would have liked, in the various Commissions connected with the British Army. A Dr. Sutherland became her means of communication with the outside world. As the years slipped by she became on closer terms with her family again, nursing Parthe when her arthritis was crippling and taking care of her mother in her old age, but still she tried to retain her independence of them.

Far from feeling inflated about her achievements, for many years she criticised herself, bemoaned her lonely state and often fell victim to depression no doubt caused by her bodily weakness. Happily, this phase passed and she gained pleasure from her various friendships, particularly that of Benjamin Jowelt, a renowned scholar. He strenuously tried to encourage her '. . . nobody knows how many lives are saved by your nurses in hospitals; how many thousand soldiers who would have fallen victims to bad air, bad drainage and ventilation, are now alive owing to your forethought and diligence; how many natives of India . . . have been preserved from famine, oppression and the load of debt by the energy of a sick lady who can scarcely rise from her bed.'

For Florence the main struggles were over. Happiness which eluded her in earlier times at last marked her final years. 'There is so much to live for. I have lost much in failures and disappointments, as well as in grief, but, do you know, life is more precious to me now in my old age.' Although many of her contemporaries had passed away, she gained a great deal of comfort and interest from the company of young relatives and nursing friends. She continued to dominate her household staff under her sight began to fail. Two honours were heaped upon her when she was almost too old to appreciate their significance, the Order of Merit awarded to a woman for the first time by King Edward VII in 1907 and then the Freedom of the City of London the next year.

She lost the power of speech in February 1910 but lingered on until August 13th. Because of her express wishes for a simple funeral without ceremony she was buried in the family grave at East Wellow. Six British army sergeants carried her coffin. 'F.N. Born 1820. Died 1910' is the brief inscription written on the family tombstone.

Yet her lasting memorial would always be in the hearts of people whose lives had been changed or even saved by her superhuman efforts, people from all walks of life, all continents and creeds.

'The lady with the lamp' will never be forgotten in the annals of human history.